FUTURE WORLD

For a free color catalog describing Gareth Stevens' list of high-quality children's books call 1-800-433-0942.

Library of Congress Cataloging-in-Publication Data

Hillman, Susan, 1962-
      Future world.

      (Fact finders)
      Bibliography: p.
      Summary: Describes a variety of new inventions in
such fields as medicine, computers, travel, and space
technology and discusses their effect on our future lives.
      1. Technology--Juvenile literature. [1. Technology]
I. Novis, Connie, 1960-   . II Miles, John, 1960-   .
III. Johnson, Paul, 1951-   ill. IV. Title. V. Series.
T48.H495   1989   600   89-42981
ISBN 0-8368-0135-0

This North American edition first published in 1989 by

Gareth Stevens Children's Books
7317 West Green Tree Road
Milwaukee, Wisconsin 53223, USA

US edition copyright © 1989. First published in the United Kingdom with
an original text copyright © 1989 Victoria House Publishing Ltd.

Series editor: Rita Reitci
Research editor: Scott Enk

Printed in the United States of America

1 2 3 4 5 6 7 8 9 95 94 93 92 91 90 89

FACT FINDER

FUTURE WORLD

Written by S. Hillman, J. Miles, & C. Novis

Illustrated by G. Smith, P. Johnson, C. Lyon, & M. Newton

Gareth Stevens Children's Books
MILWAUKEE

FUTURE WORLD

Scientific technology is rapidly changing our everyday lives. In this book you can find out about the very latest inventions, and how they are likely to develop in the future. There are seven chapters, each one dealing with a different subject, shown below.

FUTURE COMPUTERS 6-11

Computers have already had a major impact in all sorts of different fields. In this section you can find out how they work, and how computerized robots, superfast "thinking" computers, and even computerized teachers may serve us in the future.

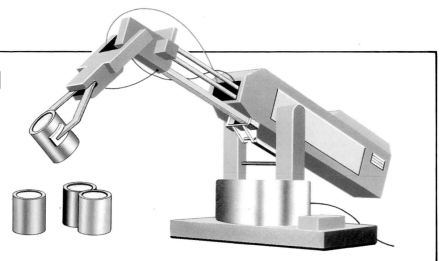

FUTURE ENERGY 12-17

In this section you can find out about the latest forms of energy, such as nuclear, solar, tidal, and wind power, and geothermal energy from hot underground springs.

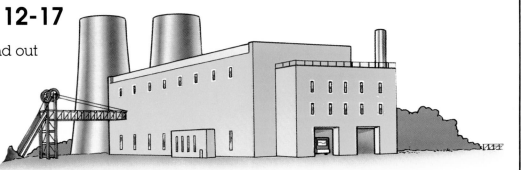

FUTURE HOMES 18-23

In this section, you can find out how today's technology might develop and alter your home. For example, in the future you might live in a computer-controlled house, with robot servants, hologram decorations, and a TV room covered with giant screens! You may be able to control all your household gadgets from outside your home.

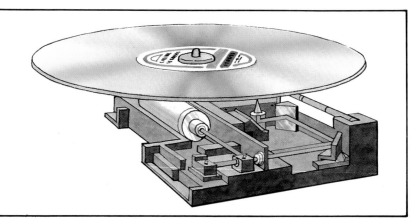

FUTURE MEDICINE 24-29

Medicine is rapidly changing, with all kinds of new scanning machines and microscopes to help physicians diagnose illnesses much more easily.

In this section you can find out how some of the latest innovations work and how medicine might improve further. For instance, you might be able to maintain your own health at home in the future by using computerized technology.

FUTURE TRAVEL 30-35

People travel more than ever before, and in the future the demand is likely to be for faster, more comfortable types of transportation.

In this section you can find out about superfast trains that don't need any wheels and futuristic cars that run on electricity, sunlight, alcohol, and even plant oil! One day, you might even travel in a space plane orbiting the Earth.

FUTURE SPACE 36-41

Already space satellites are important in our everyday lives. In this section you can find out how they work and what they are used for.

There is information on futuristic space stations and missions into deep space, perhaps to discover new planets and possibly even life forms elsewhere in the Universe.

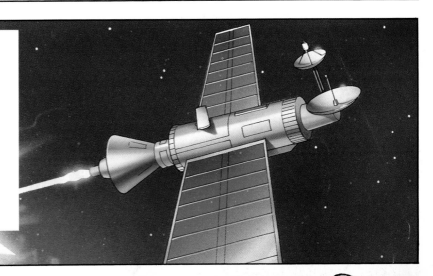

FUTURE SCIENCE 42-45

In this section you can learn about some of the newest scientific work in progress that may prove important in our future lives. For instance, superconducting materials will make electric-powered machines much cheaper and more efficient. Genetic fingerprinting will make crime detection easier, and holograms are likely to become much more common.

You can even find out about a futuristic plan to make time travel more slowly!

For easy reference, each chapter in this book has a colored strip across the top of its pages. The seven different colors are shown on the right.

pp. 6-11
pp. 12-17
pp. 18-23
pp. 24-29
pp. 30-35
pp. 36-41
pp. 42-45

FUTURE COMPUTERS

You can see computers at work in schools, homes, and offices, but the computers of the future will work faster and do more complicated tasks than any around today. Scientists are even developing computers that can think for themselves. This technology is called artificial intelligence and will play a large part in computers of the future.

HOW COMPUTERS WORK

A computer is a machine that does calculations much faster than a person can. It must have instructions telling it what to do. Changing the instructions will make the computer perform in various other ways.

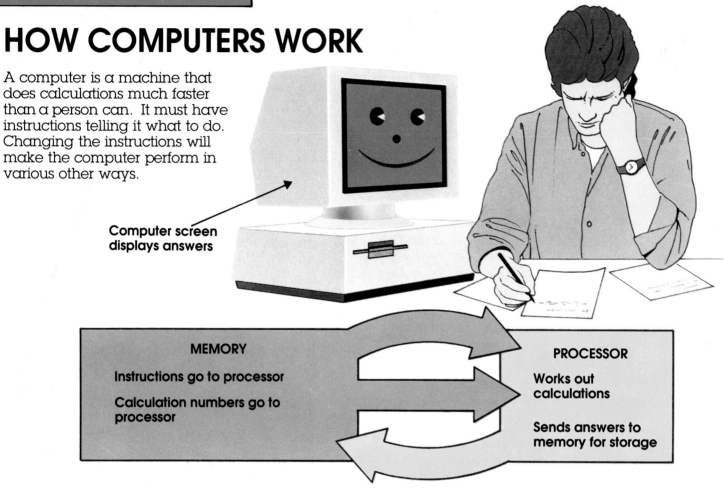

Computer screen displays answers

MEMORY		PROCESSOR
Instructions go to processor		Works out calculations
Calculation numbers go to processor		Sends answers to memory for storage

Inside every computer there is a processor and a memory. The processor is the part that carries out the instructions that are given to the computer.

The memory stores the instructions and the calculations the computer uses to get answers. It can also store the answers themselves, once they have been worked out.

PROGRAMMING

A set of computer instructions is called a program. Trained people, called programmers, write the programs. They are stored on disks, to be loaded into a computer when needed.

To obtain the results wanted, a computer must work through a program. No computerized machine can work without one. If a program contains a mistake, or a bug, the computer will not be able to function properly.

By changing the program, you can make a computer do different tasks.

Disk

USING A COMPUTER

Computers receive programs through inputs. These can be information, or data, typed in on a keyboard, or fed through a camera or microphone. When the computer has finished its task, the answers go into the memory for storage. An output, such as a printer, can retrieve the answers. Some outputs can print out pictures and some can give answers using sounds that imitate the human voice.

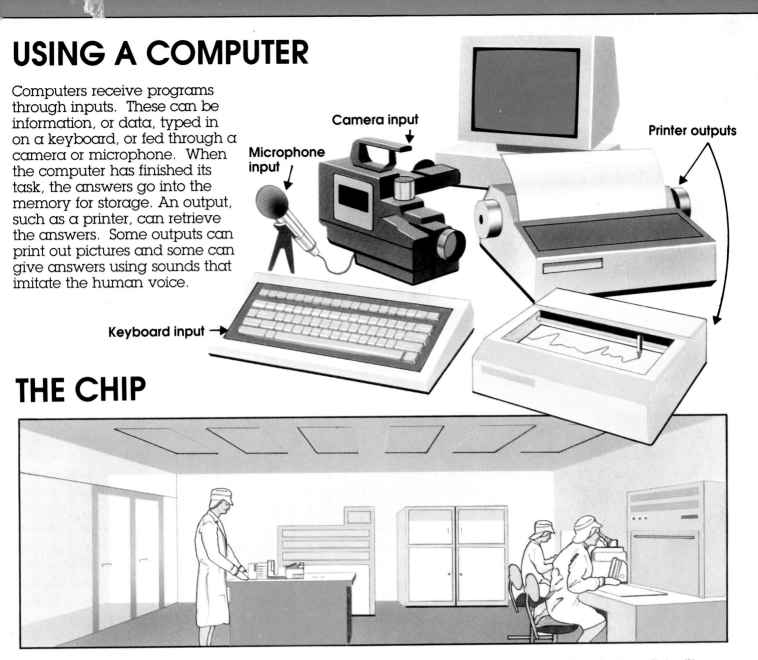

Camera input

Microphone input

Printer outputs

Keyboard input

THE CHIP

Computer processors and memories consist of a material called silicon. Manufacturers make thin wafers from silicon. They then cut these wafers into silicon chips.

To avoid contamination by dust or dirt, silicon chip manufacture takes place in very clean, sterilized rooms. These rooms are about 1,000 times cleaner than hospital operating rooms.

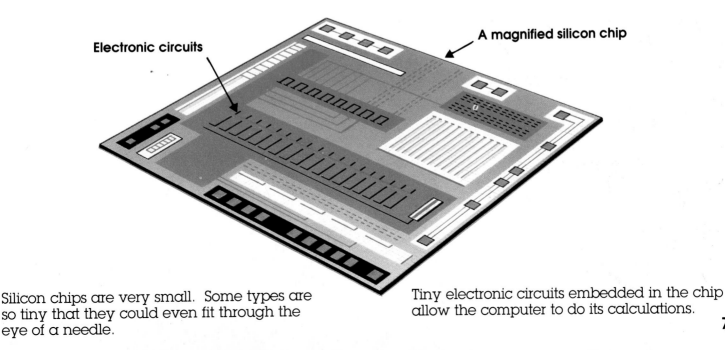

Electronic circuits

A magnified silicon chip

Silicon chips are very small. Some types are so tiny that they could even fit through the eye of a needle.

Tiny electronic circuits embedded in the chip allow the computer to do its calculations.

ROBOTS

Robots will play an important part in the world of the future. A robot is a machine that performs a task, directed by its computer components. Many factories use robots to perform simple, repetitive jobs, such as riveting car panels. Engineers design these robots to do one task, repeating it over and over.

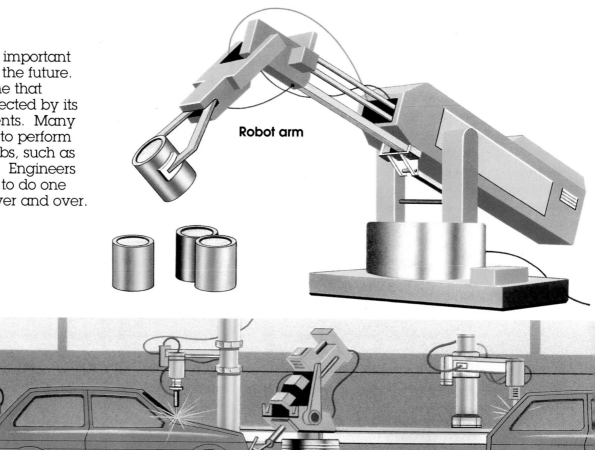

Robot arm

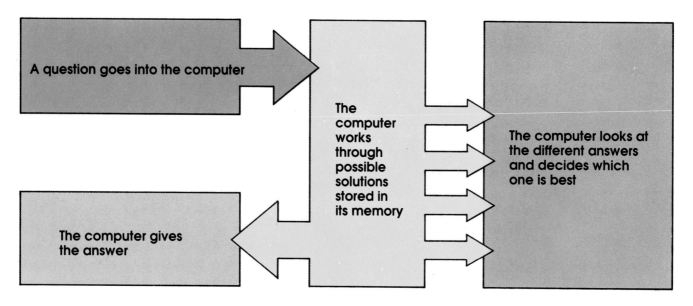

Robot factory line

In the future it will be possible for robots to run entire factories. The robots will be controlled by a powerful central computer.

A few people would check on the robots, but another computer could spot faults and alert someone when they occur.

ARTIFICIAL INTELLIGENCE

A question goes into the computer

The computer works through possible solutions stored in its memory

The computer looks at the different answers and decides which one is best

The computer gives the answer

Artificial intelligence is the name for programs that are developing that will enable computers to think for themselves.

Artificial intelligence begins with a problem loaded into a computer.

The computer can then work through a list of possible solutions stored in its memory, trying each one to see where it leads. It can look at the projected answers and decide which solution is best.

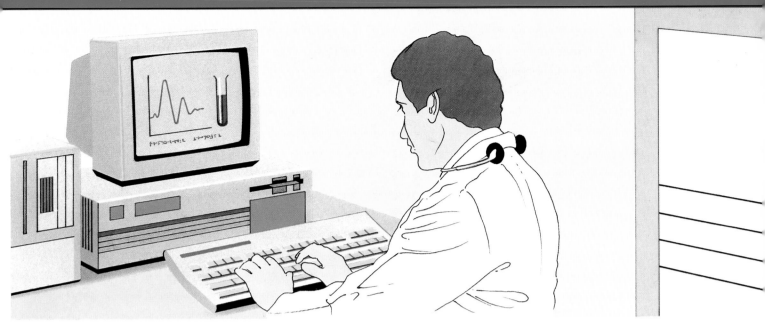

An artificial intelligence program will help doctors to find out what is wrong with a patient. The doctor would feed information on the symptoms into the computer.

The computer would scan possible diseases among data stored in its memory and select the one that fits the symptoms. It would then recommend a course of treatment to the doctor.

Some artificial intelligence programs can recognize speech or faces. The computer does this through video or microphone inputs. You can find out more about this on p. 18.

As more powerful and speedy computers appear, artificial intelligence programs will become more complex, and the future may bring more robots that can see and speak.

EXPERT SYSTEMS

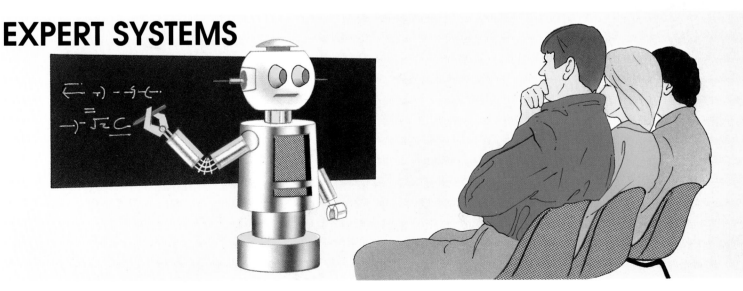

Expert systems are computers programmed with the knowledge that a human expert might possess, for instance, the doctor's system shown at the top of the page. They are likely to do more difficult tasks in the future.

There are many possibilities for expert systems. For example, people could design houses using architect systems, or perhaps clothes using fashion designer systems. Expert systems could even teach classes.

FASTER COMPUTERS

Future computers are likely to contain thousands of processors, instead of the small number inside today's machines. They will be able to do thousands of calculations at once.

These parallel processing computers will be able to work much faster than today's models because of the many extra processors inside. They will be much more powerful tools.

A calculation that might take many years on one of today's computers will only take a minute on a parallel processing model.

As a result, these incredibly efficient machines will be able to perform all kinds of very complex tasks.

OPTICAL COMPUTERS

Today's computers are usually electronic. This means that they do their calculations using tiny currents of electricity. In the future, supercomputers might use tiny rays of light instead of electricity.

The light can travel through fiber-optic tubes, narrow flexible rods made up of glass fibers. Since light travels a lot faster than electricity, fiber-optic computers will be able to do calculations much more quickly.

COMPUTER FACT FINDER

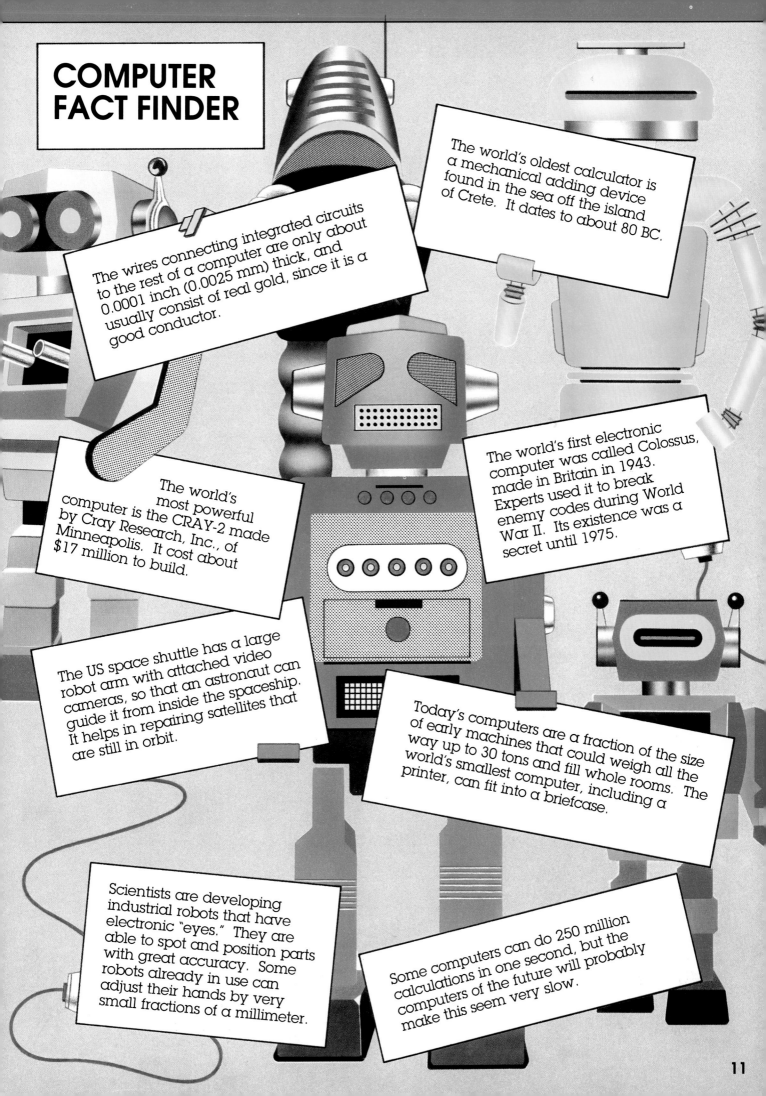

The world's oldest calculator is a mechanical adding device found in the sea off the island of Crete. It dates to about 80 BC.

The wires connecting integrated circuits to the rest of a computer are only about 0.0001 inch (0.0025 mm) thick, and usually consist of real gold, since it is a good conductor.

The world's most powerful computer is the CRAY-2 made by Cray Research, Inc., of Minneapolis. It cost about $17 million to build.

The world's first electronic computer was called Colossus, made in Britain in 1943. Experts used it to break enemy codes during World War II. Its existence was a secret until 1975.

The US space shuttle has a large robot arm with attached video cameras, so that an astronaut can guide it from inside the spaceship. It helps in repairing satellites that are still in orbit.

Today's computers are a fraction of the size of early machines that could weigh all the way up to 30 tons and fill whole rooms. The world's smallest computer, including a printer, can fit into a briefcase.

Scientists are developing industrial robots that have electronic "eyes." They are able to spot and position parts with great accuracy. Some robots already in use can adjust their hands by very small fractions of a millimeter.

Some computers can do 250 million calculations in one second, but the computers of the future will probably make this seem very slow.

FUTURE ENERGY

We use energy to run machines, and we will need much more in the future. Energy comes from many different sources, such as oil, gasoline, natural gas, and nuclear power. However, natural sources, such as gas and oil, will eventually run out, so scientists continue to search for new forms of energy to use in the future.

ELECTRICITY

Coal-fired generating station

Producing electricity requires other power sources, such as coal or oil, to run the generators that create electric current. All generators have a coil rotating inside a magnetic field. The moving coil generates an electric current.

New sources of energy must be found to replace coal and oil, as the demand for electricity grows. One answer is nuclear energy, already used to power electric generators in many countries.

NUCLEAR ENERGY

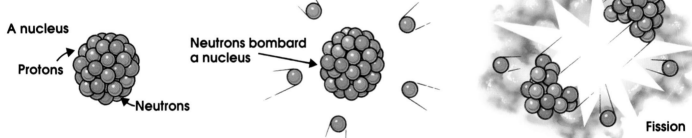

A nucleus

Protons

Neutrons

Neutrons bombard a nucleus

Fission

All materials consist of tiny building blocks called atoms. In the center, each atom has a nucleus (plural: nuclei), made up of proton and, usually, neutron particles. The nucleus is surrounded by particles called electrons.

Some atoms give off streams of particles called radiation. These atoms can be split apart in a process called fission. In nuclear power stations, neutrons bombard radioactive nuclei until they split.

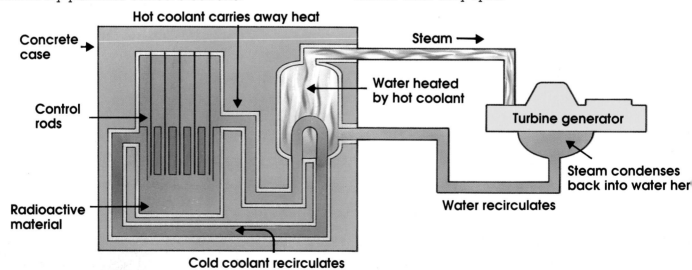

Hot coolant carries away heat

Concrete case

Control rods

Radioactive material

Steam →

Water heated by hot coolant

Turbine generator

Steam condenses back into water her

Water recirculates

Cold coolant recirculates

Fission gives off a large amount of heat. In a nuclear power station, controlled fission gives off enough heat to boil water.

The steam from the boiling water then drives an electricity-producing turbine. You can see the process above.

TURBINES

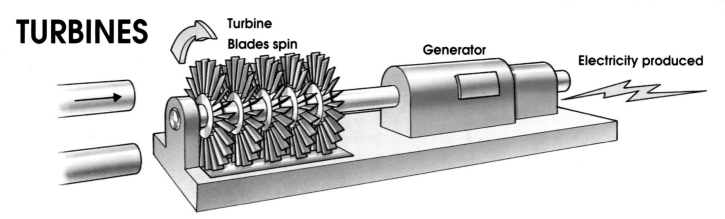

Turbine Blades spin

Generator

Electricity produced

A turbine is a rotating shaft with blades attached to it. The steam from the nuclear system rushes past the blades, making them spin around, just like a windmill in the wind.

The turbines are connected to generators. The spinning blades power the generators to produce an electric current that can be sent through wires to our homes.

RADIOACTIVE DANGERS

It is difficult to find safe places to dispose of nuclear waste once it has been created, and exposure to radioactive material is very dangerous. The waste can remain dangerous for hundreds, and even thousands, of years.

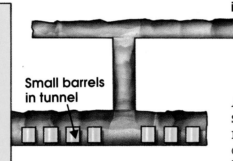

Radioactive waste stored underground in unused mines

Small barrels in tunnel

At this time, radioactive waste is put into sealed barrels and buried, often in disused mineshafts, or sunk in the deep sea. The yellow and black sign, shown on the left, is put on the barrels to show that they are dangerous.

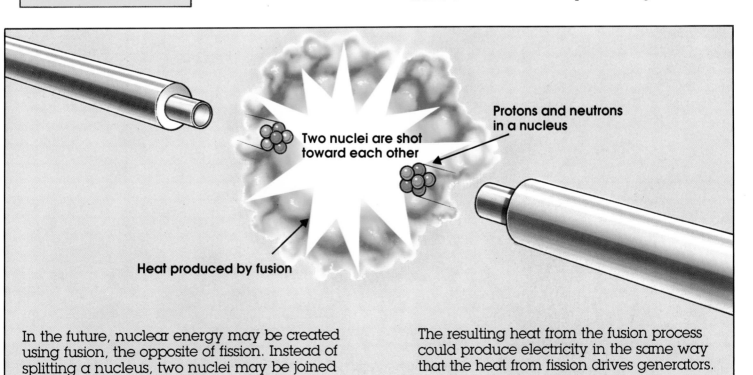

Two nuclei are shot toward each other

Protons and neutrons in a nucleus

Heat produced by fusion

In the future, nuclear energy may be created using fusion, the opposite of fission. Instead of splitting a nucleus, two nuclei may be joined together to create heat.

The resulting heat from the fusion process could produce electricity in the same way that the heat from fission drives generators.

WIND ENERGY

The wind is another source of energy that can be used to generate electricity. Wind energy is not a new idea. For many centuries, wind has powered windmills for grinding grain.

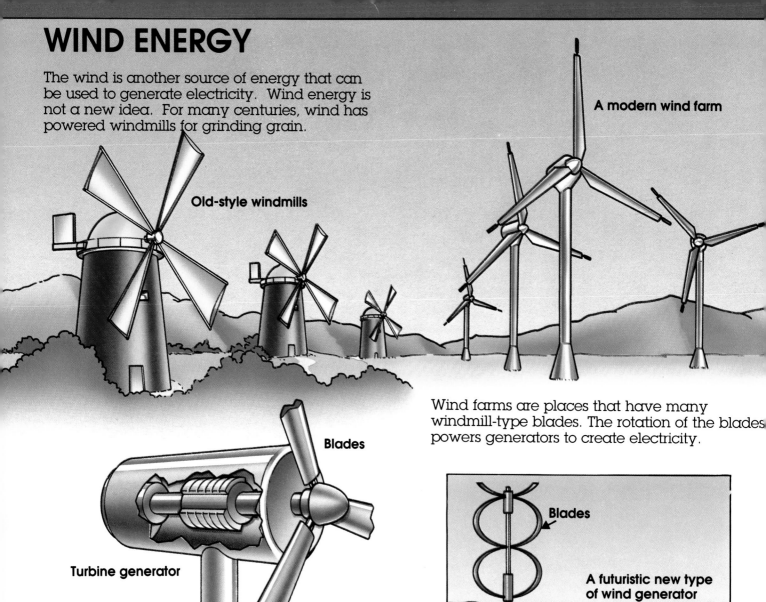

Old-style windmills

A modern wind farm

Blades

Turbine generator

Wind farms are places that have many windmill-type blades. The rotation of the blades powers generators to create electricity.

Blades

A futuristic new type of wind generator

The blades of a modern windmill connect to a wind turbine. When the turbine turns, it powers a generator. Unfortunately, it will only operate when the wind blows.

Scientists are developing blades that need very little wind to drive them. But it takes a large number of blades to produce a usable amount of power, taking up a lot of space.

SOLAR ENERGY

Solar energy comes from sunlight. Solar cells can convert it into electricity. These cells can power everyday items, such as watches, stereos, and calculators.

Solar cells

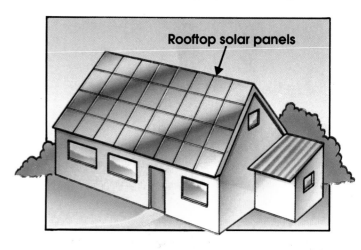

Rooftop solar panels

Some houses have solar panels that collect the Sun's energy to heat up liquid flowing through pipes beneath the panels. The hot liquid flows through a machine called a heat exchanger that extracts the heat. The stored heat is then used to heat the house as needed.

Solar panels cover the roof of a school in Atlanta, Georgia

The panels power the heating in Winter, and the air conditioning in Summer

Large factories and schools can run on solar heating, if they have many rooftop solar panels. Experimental solar power stations have produced electricity, but just during the daytime when the Sun is out.

One solution is to build solar power stations in space, where the Sun shines all the time. The stations would be reflecting dishes several miles across. The energy they produce would beam down to Earth for conversion to electricity.

TIDAL ENERGY

In the future, the sea could be a valuable source of energy. The movements of tides and waves could be harnessed to a generator to produce electricity, as shown below.

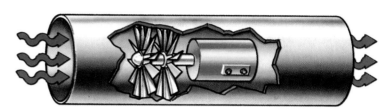

Incoming tide — gates open at its highest level

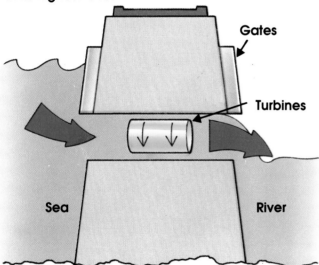

Gates

Turbines

Sea

River

Outgoing tide — gates open at its lowest level

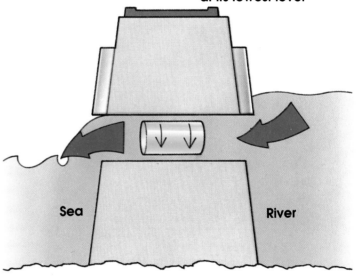

Sea

River

An estuary is the mouth of a river where sea tides meet the river's current. Estuary dams can generate electricity by making use of the changing level of the tides.

This dam has movable sluice gates. Raising the gates lets water pass through. Lowering the gates holds it back. When the tide is rising, the sluice gates stay shut. Water builds up on the sea side of the dam, but the estuary remains shallow.

When the tide reaches its highest point, the sluice gates lift up. The water built up on the sea side now rushes into the estuary. As it passes through the dam, it spins a turbine that drives an electric generator.

When the water on both sides is level, the sluice gates lower. As the tide goes out, the water level on the sea side drops. Then the sluice gates open, and the turbines spin as the estuary water floods back into the sea.

GEOTHERMAL ENERGY

An enormous store of energy lies beneath the Earth's surface. Some deep layers of rock in the Earth's crust are very hot. At the Earth's center, the temperature is believed to be 8,100°F (4,500°C). Energy from deep inside the Earth is called geothermal energy.

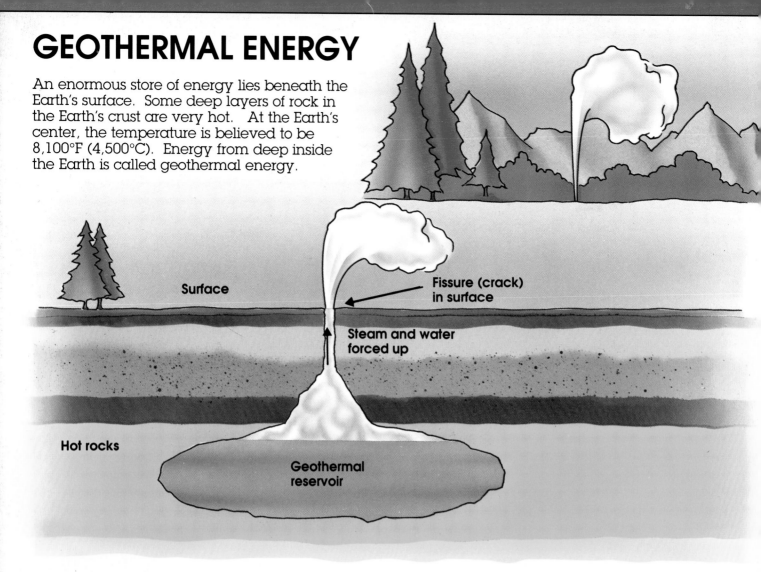

Surface

Fissure (crack) in surface

Steam and water forced up

Hot rocks

Geothermal reservoir

Geysers are one form of geothermal energy. They are large spouts of hot water and steam that force their way up through cracks in the Earth's crust.

They come from geothermal reservoirs, huge underground lakes of boiling water thousands of feet beneath the land surface. They occur in areas of volcanic activity.

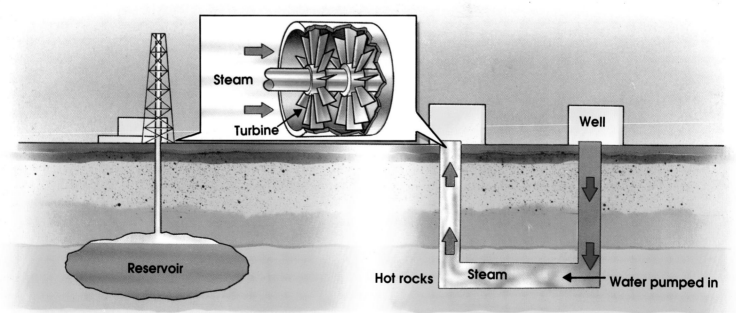

Steam

Turbine

Well

Reservoir

Hot rocks

Steam

Water pumped in

Drilling a well deep down to a geothermal reservoir will create an artificial geyser. The steam from the boiling water underground rushes up to the surface through the well, spinning a turbine that is connected to an electric generator (see p. 13).

Engineers without a geothermal reservoir make a geyser by drilling two wells close together deep down into hot rocks. Water pumped into one well heats up from the rocks. The steam goes up the second well, driving a turbine and generator.

(see p. 13)

FUTURE ENERGY FACT FINDER

Scientists are experimenting with ways of deriving energy from the waves. One method is to use floats called bobbing ducks. They bob up and down on the waves, and the movement drives a generator to produce electricity.

The world's largest nuclear power station is in Fukushima, Japan. It can produce over 9,000 megawatts of power. The most powerful power station is that of Grand Coulee Dam in Washington State.

The world's biggest solar energy furnace is in California. It uses almost 2,000 mirrors that focus the Sun's rays onto a boiler unit on top of a tower. This produces steam that drives electricity-generating turbines.

The treatment of sewage yields a gas called methane. Many sewage treatment plants collect the methane and use it to make their own electricity for lighting and heating.

In India, cow dung is used for energy. Millions of tons are dried each year for use as fuel, just like wood or coal. North American Indians used buffalo dung, called buffalo chips, for their heating and cooking fuel.

The world's most powerful wind generators can produce thousands of kilowatts of electricity. One example is the MOD-5A turbine on the northern shore of Oahu, Hawaii. It is designed to produce over 7,000 kilowatts when the wind reaches 32 mph (50 kph).

The hot water and steam from geysers can be used for heating. In Iceland, it is used to heat homes and offices in the capital city of Reykjavik.

FUTURE HOMES

In the future, you are likely to find more and more modern technology in your home designed for making life easier and safer.

Computers of the future may actually run the systems in our homes. For example, programs enable them to control heating and lighting.

COMPUTER DOORS

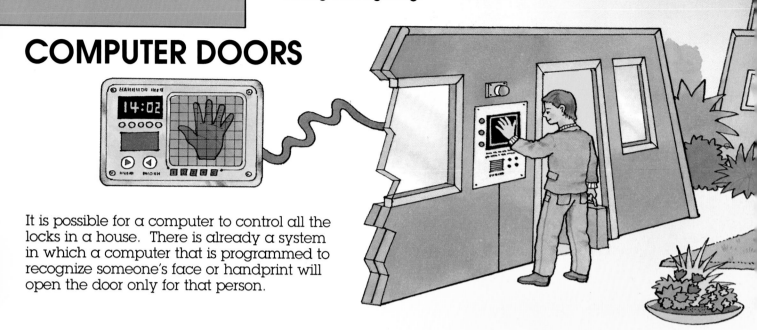

It is possible for a computer to control all the locks in a house. There is already a system in which a computer that is programmed to recognize someone's face or handprint will open the door only for that person.

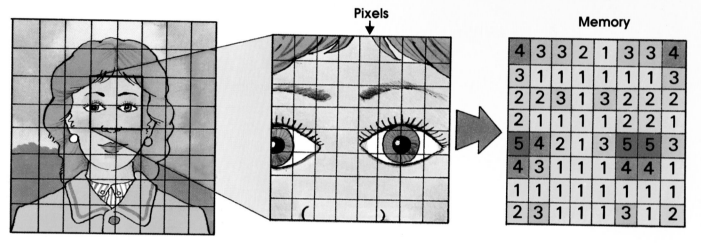

To open a computer-controlled door you must put your face or hand in front of a video camera. The camera signal travels to the computer, which converts it into a picture made up of many tiny squares called pixels.

Each square is given a number according to how light or dark it appears. The computer compares the number pattern to numbers in its memory representing a recognized face or hand. If they match, the door will open.

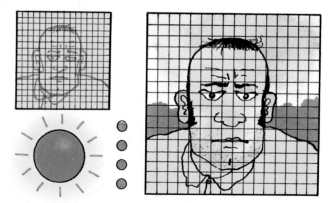

If strangers tried to enter, the computer could record and store their pictures. This could be useful for finding out who has called and could even catch burglars.

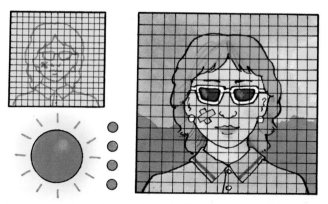

One unsolved problem is that computers find it difficult to recognize hands and faces when they alter. Eyeglasses and bandages change a face, and rings alter a hand.

THE COMPUTER HOUSE

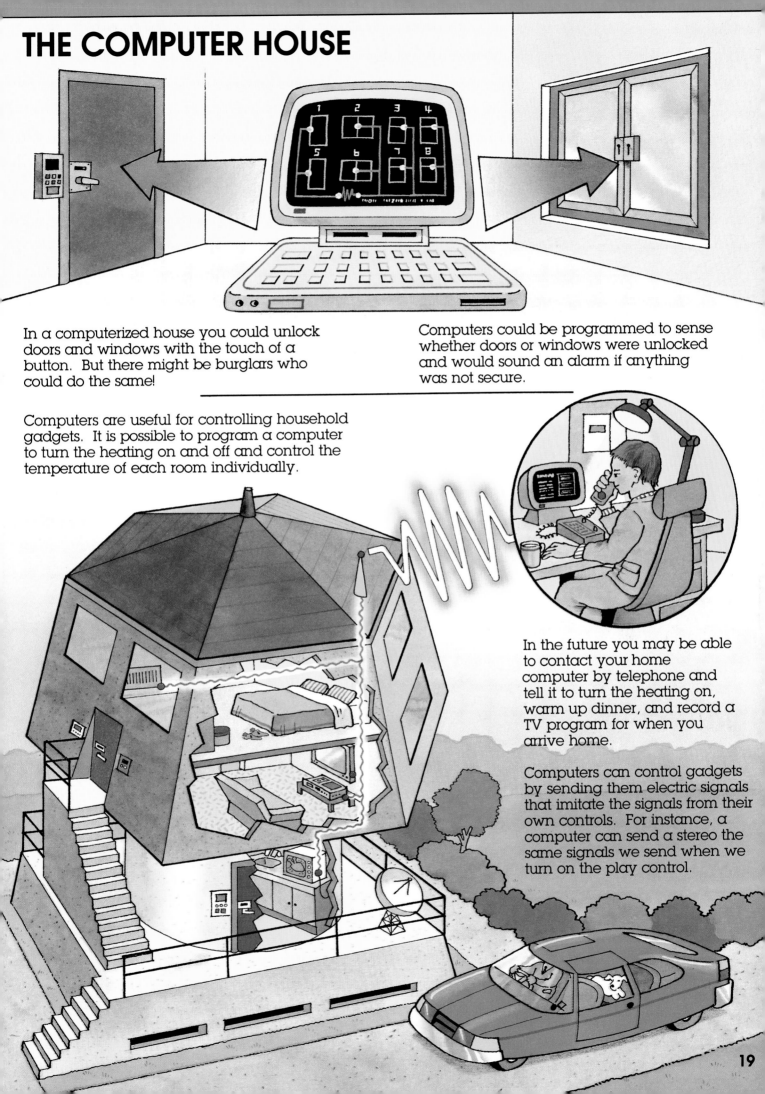

In a computerized house you could unlock doors and windows with the touch of a button. But there might be burglars who could do the same!

Computers could be programmed to sense whether doors or windows were unlocked and would sound an alarm if anything was not secure.

Computers are useful for controlling household gadgets. It is possible to program a computer to turn the heating on and off and control the temperature of each room individually.

In the future you may be able to contact your home computer by telephone and tell it to turn the heating on, warm up dinner, and record a TV program for when you arrive home.

Computers can control gadgets by sending them electric signals that imitate the signals from their own controls. For instance, a computer can send a stereo the same signals we send when we turn on the play control.

HOME ENTERTAINMENT

In the future, TV screens could cover an entire wall, or even fill up all the walls of a room to make you seem part of the action.

Because of the way they work, today's TV screens cannot be very large, but there may be ways of solving this problem.

Tiny dots make up a TV picture

Stadium screen picture

Light-emitting diodes

A TV picture is made up of very tiny dots, so small that they are only visible from very close up. If a TV screen were made ten times bigger, the dots would also be ten times bigger, spoiling the image on the screen.

Some very large screens are used in stadiums. They create a picture out of colored light emitted from thousands of electric devices called diodes. The future may see such screens in homes.

It is now possible to have a hologram in your home. Holograms are 3-D pictures made using laser lights and mirrors. You can find out more about them on p. 44.

No one has yet invented motion picture holograms, but one day they may be possible.

If moving holograms were combined with recorded music, you could have a 3-D orchestra or rock group playing in front of you!

Holograms could be used to decorate a room. For instance, you could have a hologram of a valuable antique or a painting.

FUTURE SOUND

Now you can get high-quality sound in your home using compact discs. Sound equipment will develop even further than this in the future.

1. To record a compact disc (CD), a microphone converts music into an electric signal made up of electrons (see p. 42). They produce an electric current when they pass through solid material.

(see p. 42)

2. The electrons flow through an electronic circuit. Loud music causes a big signal — the electrons flow quickly. Soft music causes a small signal — the electrons flow slowly.

Code is transferred to disc

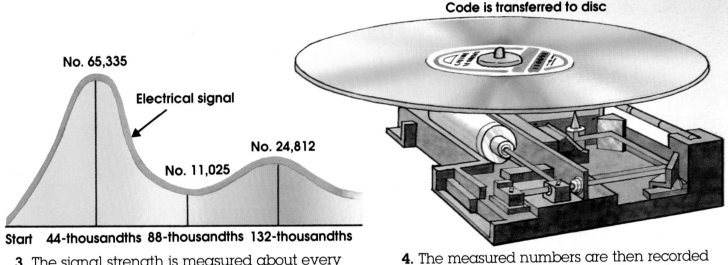

No. 65,335

Electrical signal

No. 24,812

No. 11,025

Start   44-thousandths   88-thousandths   132-thousandths

3. The signal strength is measured about every 44-thousandths of a second. It is registered as a number. The weakest signal gets the number 1. The loudest signal gets a number over 60,000.

4. The measured numbers are then recorded onto the surface of a disc in the form of a code of dimples and flat surfaces, starting at the center and spiraling outward.

5. When the disc is played, it spins around and a laser beam follows the path of the spiral.

A light sensor reads the dimples and flat surfaces, monitoring the way that the light from the laser bounces off the disc. A flat surface bounces the light straight back, and a dimple scatters the light.

By reading the code, the CD player can work out the numbers used to measure the original signal and reconstruct the music.

Laser   Sensor

Flat disc surface

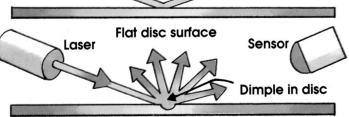

Laser   Sensor

Dimple in disc

21

FUTURE KITCHENS

Machines now do washing and cooking, but kitchens will be more automated in the future.

Kitchens may well be designed so robots can work in them. There might even be pre-packed meal kits that robots could prepare. There are already some butler robots in use. These robots can serve meals and drinks to their owners.

Many people now have microwave ovens. These may completely replace ordinary stoves in the future. In ordinary stoves, food cooks by being close to heat. Microwave ovens are different. They generate heat from inside the food.

Ordinary oven　　**Microwave oven**

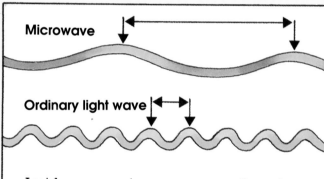

Microwave

Ordinary light wave

Inside every microwave oven there is a magnetron that converts electricity into microwaves, that is, electromagnetic radiation with a much longer wavelength than ordinary visible light.

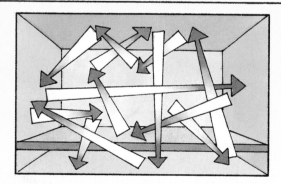

The microwaves travel into the oven where food is placed. The oven walls are metal and they reflect the microwaves, just like a mirror reflects light. When food is placed in the oven, microwaves hit it from all directions as they bounce off the metal walls.

Microwaves cannot travel very far through food. They stop soon after they have penetrated it. When they stop, their energy is converted into heat, making the food hot very quickly. Microwave ovens can cook food in a fraction of the normal time.

FUTURE HOMES FACT FINDER

Heat- and light-sensitive computers can close window blinds to block out sunlight if a room gets too warm, or when it gets dark outside.

Bubble houses have proven successful in trials. They are made out of a plastic skin inflated with an air pump. If you lived in a bubble home, you could take it with you when you moved!

Underground homes have appeared as a way of saving building space. Windows in the roof let in the sunlight from above.

Some computers can identify people by the sounds of their voices, as well as visually. They can measure sound waves, and compare them to recognized voiceprints.

There are many futuristic house designs. The picture on this page is from an idea by the US architect Frank Lloyd Wright.

Compact disc videos combine high-quality sounds and pictures. In the future, compact disc holograms could be developed.

A computer already exists that can identify 16 human faces, whatever the expression or angle. It takes 15 seconds to scan the face and identify it.

FUTURE MEDICINE

Medicine is a fast-moving field of science, with new operations, drugs, and tests appearing all the time. Many things that once seemed impossible are now achieved with the aid of modern technology, such as computers and lasers.

DIAGNOSIS

Before making someone feel better, a doctor must make a diagnosis to find out what the problem is. Usually the doctor asks questions and checks anything unusual. If the doctor is still unsure, there are many tests to find out more. Some of the tests that have a place in future medicine are shown below.

NMR SCANS

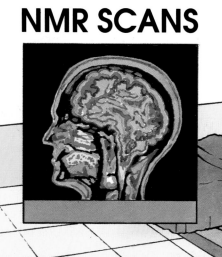

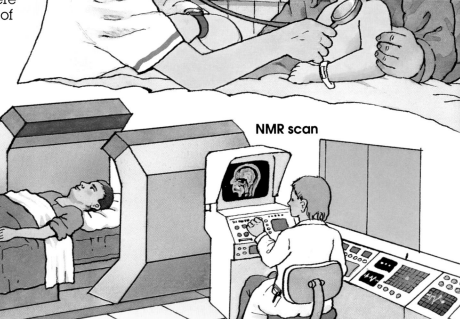

NMR scan

Nuclear magnetic resonance machines have powerful magnets that can energize different parts of the body.

When the magnets are turned off, the body emits signals that build up into a picture when measured.

CAT SCANS

CAT (computerized axial tomography) scan machines work by taking photographs of someone's body from many different angles.

A computer then builds up a complete picture that is more detailed than an x-ray because it is three-dimensional.

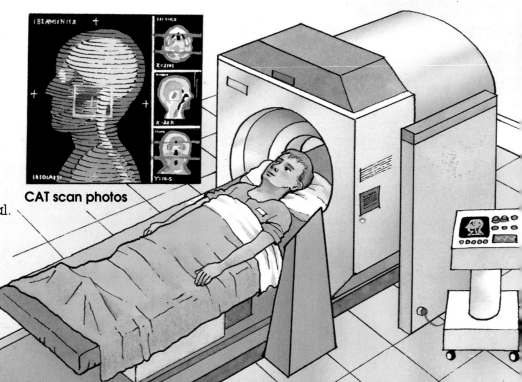

CAT scan photos

CAT scan

NUCLEAR MEDICINE

Lung image

Medical workers can use radiation (see p. 12) to good effect. They can give a patient a radioactive chemical that tends to go to one part of the body. For instance, a patient can inhale radioactive gas into the lungs. A camera picks up the radiation and constructs an image from it.

ULTRASOUND

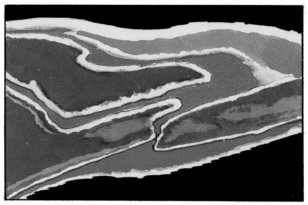

Ultrasound image

In ultrasound tests, very high-frequency sound waves travel through a part of the body. Sections of the body reflect the waves to different degrees. Experts use the measurements of these reflections to construct an image. Doctors occasionally use ultrasound to examine unborn babies.

PETT SCANS

Positron emission transaxial tomography (PETT) scans are complicated procedures often used in medical research. Besides showing the location of a body part, they actually show that part at work. For instance, they can show a heart beating. With a PETT scan, a doctor can see if the heart is functioning in the way that it should.

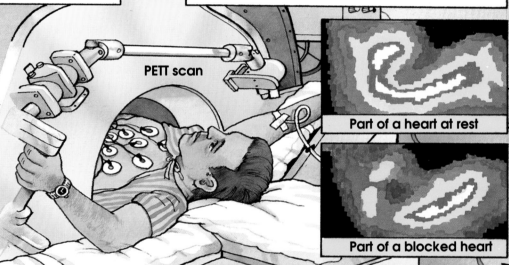

PETT scan

Part of a heart at rest

Part of a blocked heart

EKG

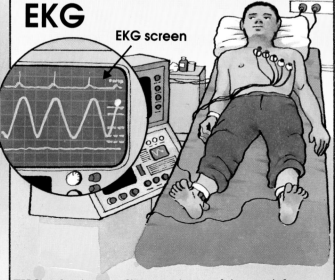

EKG screen

EKG (electrocardiogram) machines pick up the heart's pattern of electrical activity. Every heartbeat sends out a small electric wave that is displayed on a screen so experts can examine how the heart is working.

ENDOSCOPY

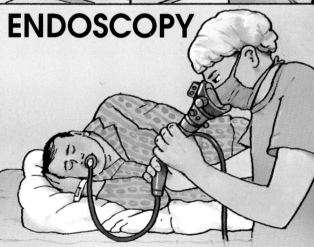

Doctors can now use a telescope-like machine called an endoscope to look inside the body. In this way, they can often diagnose illnesses without having to operate first. Sometimes the endoscope can help in treating injuries, such as damaged knees.

VACCINATION

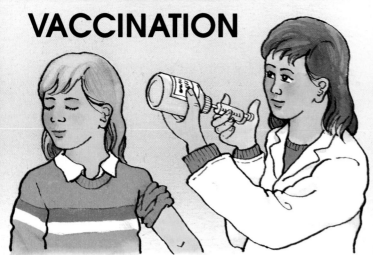

Scientists are developing new vaccines all the time to prevent diseases caused by viruses and bacteria. A vaccine makes the body think it has an infection, so it builds up the weapons to fight it. Then if the body comes in contact with the real infection, it can fight it off.

ARTIFICIAL BLOOD

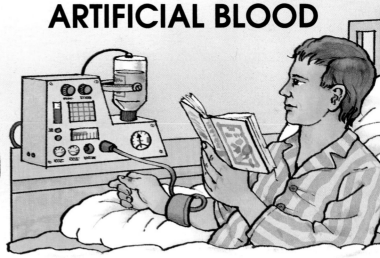

If you lose blood, your body replaces it. But sometimes you may need an extra blood transfusion for this purpose. At times there are shortages of blood. Scientists are developing an artificial form of blood to solve the problem.

PACEMAKERS

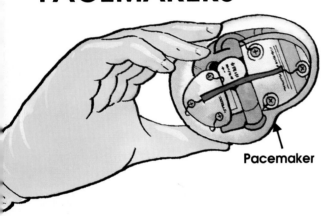

Pacemaker

Normally the heart beats at a regular rate, but sometimes the beat may slow down too much. However, a small electrical pacemaker can deliver shocks that stimulate the heart to beat properly. Nuclear batteries power some pacemakers and automatically trigger the heart only when necessary.

INFUSION PUMPS

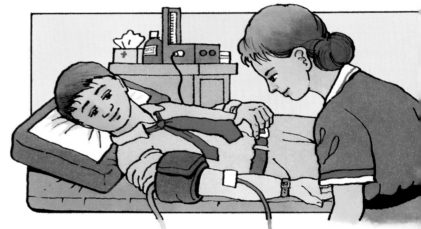

Some medicines are most effective when given in small continual doses, instead of large amounts every few hours. Now, battery-driven pumps can constantly deliver small amounts of a medicine to patients, freeing them from regular injections.

GENETIC ENGINEERING

Some chemicals in the human body are so complicated that they cannot be made in a laboratory. The formula for these chemicals is contained in a code called a gene, found inside each single cell.

Scientists have already taken certain genes and put them into bacteria or viruses. When the bacteria or viruses begin to reproduce, they follow the pattern of the new genes now inside them, instead of their own normal pattern. This is called genetic engineering. Experts now make the vaccine against smallpox this way.

SURGERY

Surgical microscope

As technology improves, surgeons can operate on smaller, more delicate parts of the body, such as eyes. These operations require absolutely accurate surgery. A surgeon needs a special microscope to see the work he must do.

ESWL

ESWL (extracorporeal sound wave lithotripsy) uses high-frequency sound waves to shatter kidney stones and gallstones within the body. The patient must be in a bath, since water helps to carry the sound.

JOINTS

Artificial joint

Joint replacements are a successful modern operation. However, scientists are trying to improve on the artificial ones now in use, to make them last much longer.

LASERS

Doctors can now use laser beams to cut very delicate tissues, or sometimes to destroy dangerous cells. They can even use them to clear heart blockages or to operate on the eye, one of the body's most delicate mechanisms.

ASEPSIS

Surgeons must keep themselves and the operation in progress as clean as possible. They scrub their hands many times and wear surgical gowns and masks. At times they need to perform an asepsis operation, one that is ultra-clean. The surgeons dress up in outfits like spacesuits and operate beneath a sterile plastic tent.

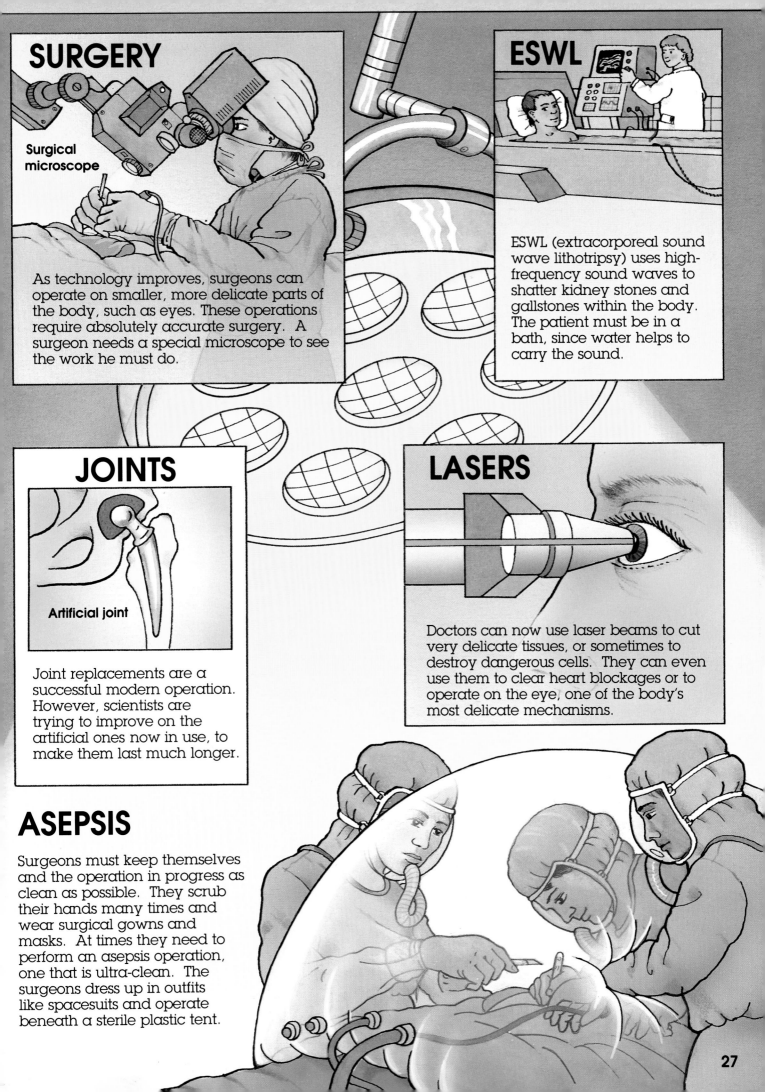

ICUs

Medical advances now cure many people. At critical times some patients need constant specialized care. Then they are cared for in ICUs (intensive care units) that contain a vast array of monitors, machines, and computers. These help the medical staff keep a close check on the patients.

ICU in operation

HOME MEDICINE

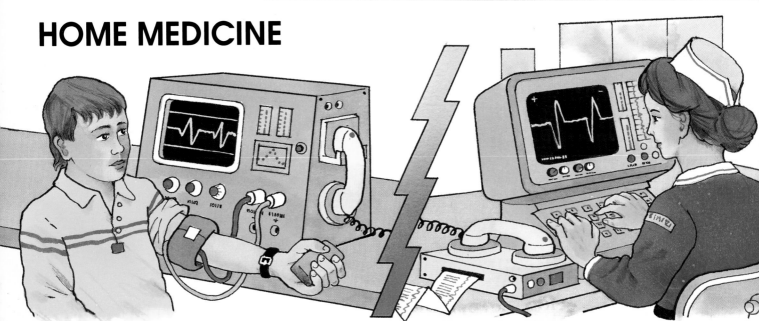

Going to a hospital for a test may not always be necessary in the future. You can already take an EKG test at home (see p. 25). The result goes in coded form by telephone line to a hospital, where it is analyzed.

You can use a computer in some home health testing. In the future, this may become more common and will help to prevent illnesses by picking up any early warning signs.

FUTURE MEDICINE FACT FINDER

The largest stone ever removed from a patient reportedly was a gallstone that weighed nearly 14 pounds (6.3 kg).
No one has ever tested whether ESWL sound waves could work on stones of this size.

The magnets used in NMR scans (see p. 24) are so powerful that anyone entering the scan room must remove metal objects from their pockets. Otherwise the magnets would be likely to tear them out!

The technique of replacing lost limbs goes back to wooden and metal legs over 2,000 years ago.
Now surgeons find it possible to control an artificial limb by using the body's existing nerve impulses.

Acupuncture is an effective painkilling technique that can take the place of anesthesia. With tiny needles inserted in special points of the body, a person having an operation stays awake, feeling no pain.

Scientists and doctors continue to search for a cure for cancer. One future possibility is an injection of chemicals or viruses that will seek out and destroy cancerous cells without affecting a patient's healthy cells.

Robot body parts may not be far off. Along with artificial limbs, medical scientists have developed artificial ears, heart valves, blood vessels, and many other replacement parts that can be installed surgically.

The search for new medical drugs continues. Scientists are turning more and more to computers to design new drugs, using special programs to find new chemical formulas and predict their effects.

29

FUTURE TRAVEL

Travel has already changed the world during the twentieth century. Now people travel more than ever before, learning from other cultures and trading with other countries. In the future, the demand is likely to be for even faster, cheaper, and more comfortable transportation than we have now.

FUTURE TRAINS

Trains now exist that do not run on wheels. Instead, they run over a single rail without touching it. These futuristic trains are known as Maglev trains.

Maglev trains can go much faster than ordinary trains. For example, a West German Maglev (magnetic levitation) can run at 186 mph (300 kph).

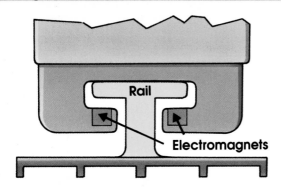

Maglev trains hover above a single rail because they are held up by electromagnets located below the track on the train itself. The electromagnets are not magnetic until they are turned on.

Turning on the track electricity activates the electromagnets and the whole train lifts upward. An electric motor then moves the Maglev train along.

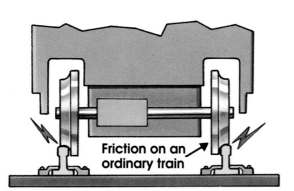

Maglev trains travel much faster than trains with wheels. They do not have to overcome the friction of wheels rubbing against rails. Friction is the resistance that surfaces have to sliding over one another. The Maglev hovers above the rail without touching any surface.

FUTURE CARS

Gasoline is processed from oil, but in the not too distant future, the Earth's supply of oil is likely to run out.

Scientists and engineers are looking for alternative ways to power cars, so that gasoline would no longer be needed.

In the future, fuel may be made from tiny plantlike organisms called algae. The algae produce oils as food reserves in the same way that a body produces fat. These oils could be converted into fuel.

Magnified algae

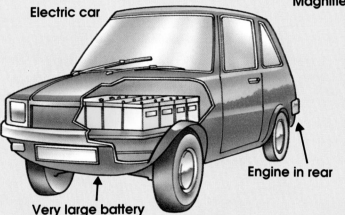

Electric car

Very large battery

Engine in rear

Electricity can power cars. Some electric cars exist, but they are not practical since the battery is too big and heavy and its electric charge does not last long enough.

A much smaller battery that stores more electricity needs to appear before electric cars are practical for everyday use.

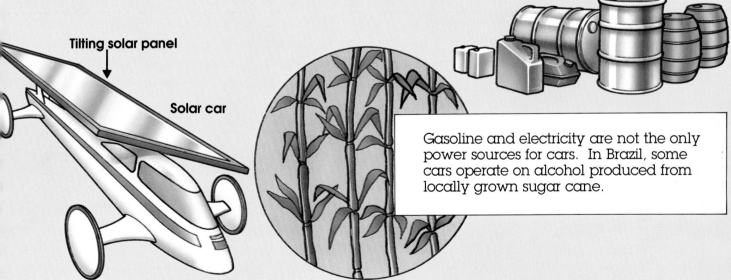

Tilting solar panel

Solar car

Gasoline and electricity are not the only power sources for cars. In Brazil, some cars operate on alcohol produced from locally grown sugar cane.

Some experimental cars use large solar panels to charge their electric batteries. Small light-sensitive cells on the panels convert the Sun's rays into electricity for the batteries. In the future, small solar-powered vehicles might become standard.

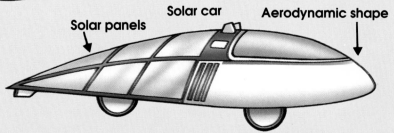

Solar panels   **Solar car**   **Aerodynamic shape**

FUTURE AIRPLANES

As demand for faster, cheaper air transportation becomes greater, engineers develop new types of airplane.

VERTICAL TAKEOFF

Harrier Jump-jet

Nozzles point down

Plane rises

Nozzles point back

Plane goes forward

Today's airliners need long runways in order to take off. However, in the future they may be able to take off and land almost vertically. Some military planes, such as the Harrier Jump-jet, already have this ability. It works by having four nozzles direct the plane's thrust.

When the Harrier takes off, its four nozzles point straight down. The engine forces a jet of hot gases down through the nozzles, lifting the plane up. When airborne, the Harrier points its nozzles to its rear so it can fly forward.

TILT-ROTOR AIRPLANES

Another type of vertical takeoff and landing aircraft uses tilt-rotors, large propellers that can be tilted horizontally or vertically. When the airplane takes off, the rotor blades are horizontal. The plane lifts up like a helicopter.

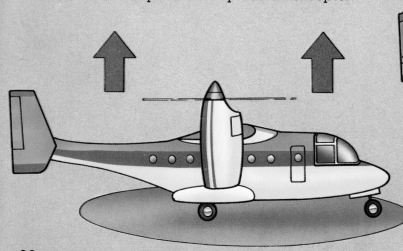

Once the airplane is aloft, the rotors tilt so that the propellers are vertical. Now the airplane flies forward.

DESIGN CHANGES

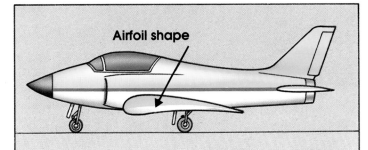

Airfoil shape

The airplanes of today rely on the air to lift them off the ground and support their wings when they are airborne. In order to fly this way, the upper wing surfaces are curved into an airfoil shape.

When an airplane flies, air rushes toward the wing. Some of the air goes over the wing and some goes underneath.

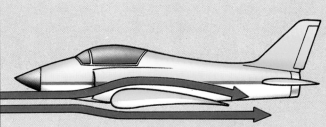

Air traveling above and below a wing

The air going over the wing goes farther and faster than the air going under the wing. The pressure of air drops as it goes faster.

The air moving under the wing is slower than the air above it, so it has greater pressure and it pushes the plane upward. In order to stay up, an airplane must travel fast enough for the upward force of air pressure to balance the downward force of the airplane's weight.

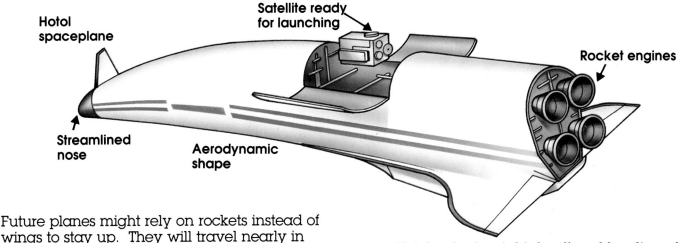

Hotol spaceplane

Satellite ready for launching

Rocket engines

Streamlined nose

Aerodynamic shape

Future planes might rely on rockets instead of wings to stay up. They will travel nearly in space, and will orbit the Earth. Someday they could carry paying passengers.

Hotol, a horizontal takeoff and landing plane, is an example of a plane designed to fly in space. It has both jet and rocket engines and can take off from an ordinary runway. This plane may even launch satellites.

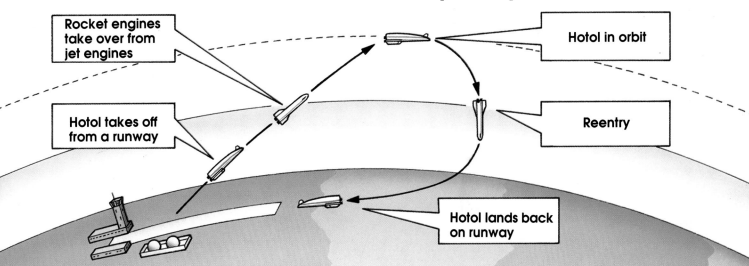

Rocket engines take over from jet engines

Hotol in orbit

Hotol takes off from a runway

Reentry

Hotol lands back on runway

Once Hotol takes off, its jet engines fly it to a height of 16 miles (26 km). At this height there is very little oxygen in the atmosphere, so its jet engines no longer function.

The rocket engines take over and fly Hotol into orbit 186 miles (300 km) high. Once its mission is complete, Hotol can reenter the Earth's atmosphere and glide to a runway.

FUTURE BICYCLES

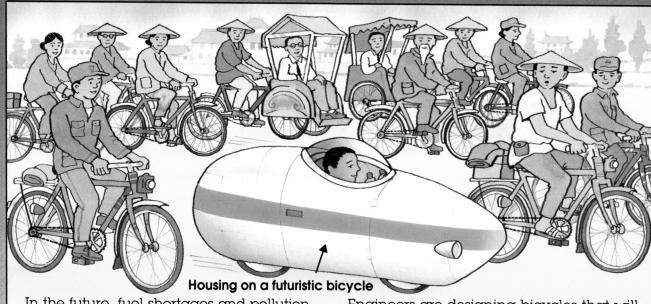

Housing on a futuristic bicycle

In the future, fuel shortages and pollution may force people to turn from cars to other forms of transportation. Faster, safer bicycle designs may become popular.

Engineers are designing bicycles that will travel at speeds of up to 45 mph (72 kph). They are streamlined, with a smooth housing that surrounds the rider.

REDUCING DRAG

To ride the new bicycle design on the right you have to lie prone. This reduces drag, a force that pushes backward on a bicycle as it travels through the air.

Most of the drag is caused by having to push air out of the way when moving forward. When the rider lies down, there is much less air to be pushed away. This eliminates most of the drag, so the bicycle can travel much faster.

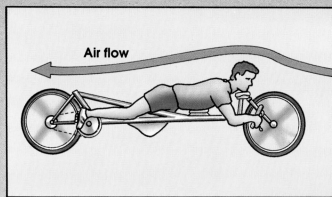

Air flow

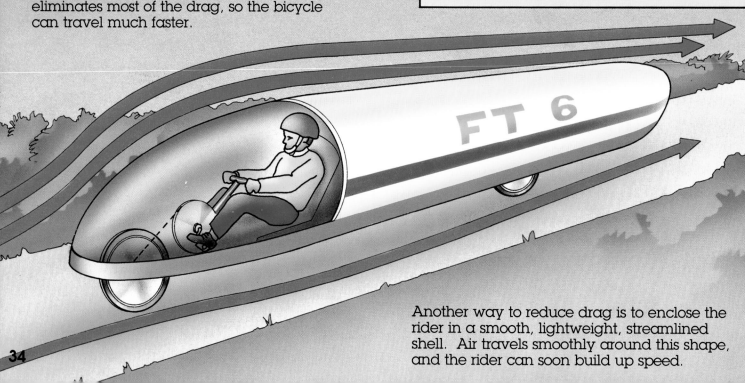

Another way to reduce drag is to enclose the rider in a smooth, lightweight, streamlined shell. Air travels smoothly around this shape, and the rider can soon build up speed.

FUTURE TRAVEL FACT FINDER

Some airplanes have wings that can swing back to form a triangular, or delta, shape. During takeoff the wings swing out to provide more lift. Then they swing back for fast flying.

Electric cars need more development before they are practical for everyday use. One early example was the Enfield. It carried a battery weighing 679 pounds (310 kg). It could travel only 40 miles (64 km) before the battery needed recharging.

TGV trains in France travel so fast that the engineer cannot see or react to the signals along the track. Instead, these trains receive messages sent along the rails and displayed in the engineer's cab. In the future, more trains will use this system.

Experts detect and track airplanes with radar. They send out radio waves and detect any that bounce back. But now military spy planes are built in special radar-avoiding shapes, out of materials that do not give off any radar signals.

Hovercraft may become more common vehicles in the future. They travel over land or water on a cushion of air. A flexible rubber skirt keeps the air from escaping, and propellers move the craft forward.

Airships are an old idea that is being reconsidered. They work by carrying a huge amount of gas that is lighter than air, allowing the ship to rise upward. Some early airships blew up because they carried flammable hydrogen gas. New airships carry helium, which does not explode.

One of the latest Japanese ship designs has sails, just like early sailing ships. But these new-style sails are made of lightweight metal. An onboard computer controls them, turning them to catch the wind.

FUTURE SPACE

Since the first satellite launch in 1957, humans have explored farther and farther into space. Already, satellites have changed our lives, making world communications much easier. The development of space shuttle-type vehicles is leading the way to permanent space stations, where colonies of people may eventually live.

SATELLITES

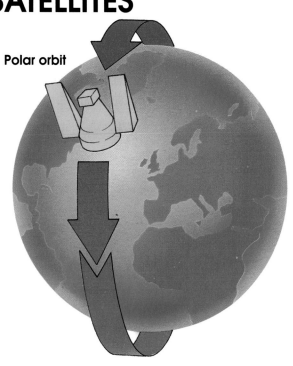

Polar orbit

Geostationary orbit

Satellite orbits depend on the craft's work. Weather satellites orbit the Earth about 14 times a day over the Poles, scanning different areas as the Earth rotates below.

Many types of satellite fly a high geostationary orbit around the Earth's Equator. They travel at the same speed that the Earth rotates, so they stay over the same area at all times.

SATELLITE PARTS

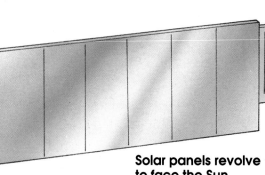

A type of communication satellite

Antenna

Top section does not spin — it carries the major equipment

Solar panels revolve to face the Sun

Spinning satellite body

Satellites do many different kinds of tasks, and they look very different from one another. But they all carry equipment for power and control. In addition, they carry special equipment to carry out their own particular job.

All satellites have an antenna to communicate with Earth. Most of them have panels of solar cells (see p. 14) that convert the Sun's radiation into electricity for power. Many of them have bodies that spin, helping to keep the satellite stable in orbit.

USEFUL SATELLITES

Satellites have many different functions. For example, they can beam TV programs around the world, monitor the weather, and help pinpoint ships for navigation.

They can collect scientific data on Earth and in space, and even spy on military targets. In the future, solar power-collecting satellites may be able to beam power to Earth (see p. 15), and satellites might have the capacity to fight wars in space.

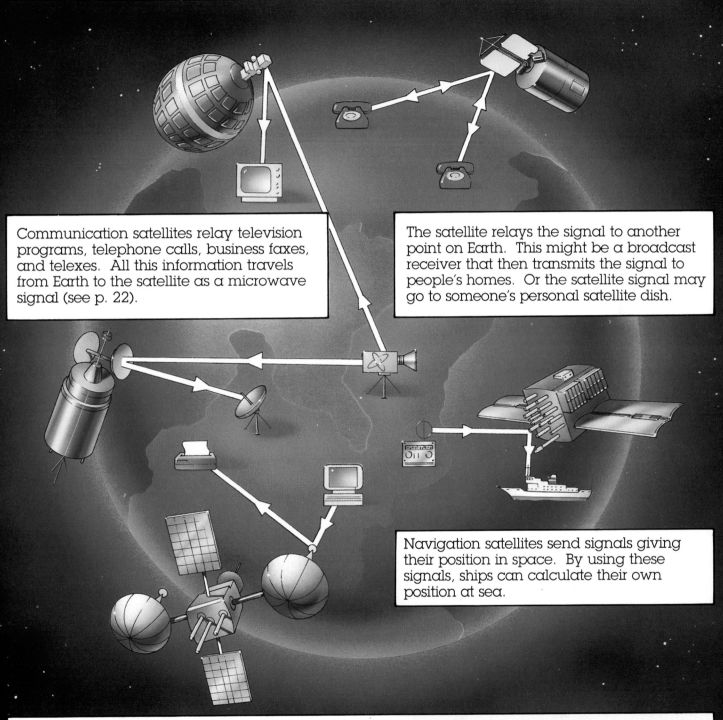

Communication satellites relay television programs, telephone calls, business faxes, and telexes. All this information travels from Earth to the satellite as a microwave signal (see p. 22).

The satellite relays the signal to another point on Earth. This might be a broadcast receiver that then transmits the signal to people's homes. Or the satellite signal may go to someone's personal satellite dish.

Navigation satellites send signals giving their position in space. By using these signals, ships can calculate their own position at sea.

Remote sensing satellites survey the Earth's surface and atmosphere. They transmit their data to Earth, where computers process it into information and pictures made up from tiny squares. Different areas of the picture are shown in different colors. For instance, plant life might be shown in different shades of red, and buildings might be blue, as shown on the right.

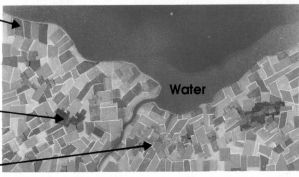

Plant life

Water

Forest

Built-up area

MILITARY SATELLITES

Over half the satellites that are launched have equipment on board for military use. For instance, communication satellites keep military bases and armies in contact, weather satellites predict weather for army exercises, and spy satellites film sensitive military areas.

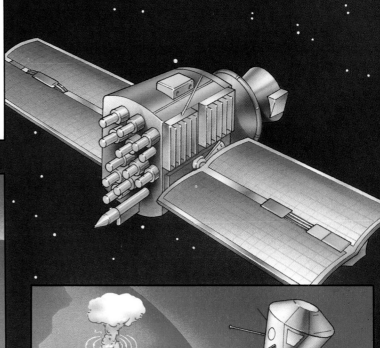

Spy satellite pictures can be very detailed. Some of them are so clear that they show people on the ground, from over 100 miles (160 km) up in space.

Spy satellites can check on nuclear bomb tests around the world, and help to enforce the treaties limiting the number of tests that can be carried out.

SATELLITE WARS

In the future there may be killer satellites, carrying weapons. They could shoot down enemy satellites or missiles using powerful laser beams, streams of concentrated light.

Some satellites could be programmed to simply blow themselves up near a space target in order to destroy it.

EXPLORING THE SOLAR SYSTEM

The Earth's atmosphere restricts our view of space. Satellites orbit above the atmosphere, so they are an ideal way of observing stars and planets.

Apart from Earth, there are eight known planets in our Solar System. In the future, satellite probes will travel to each planet and send back scientific data.

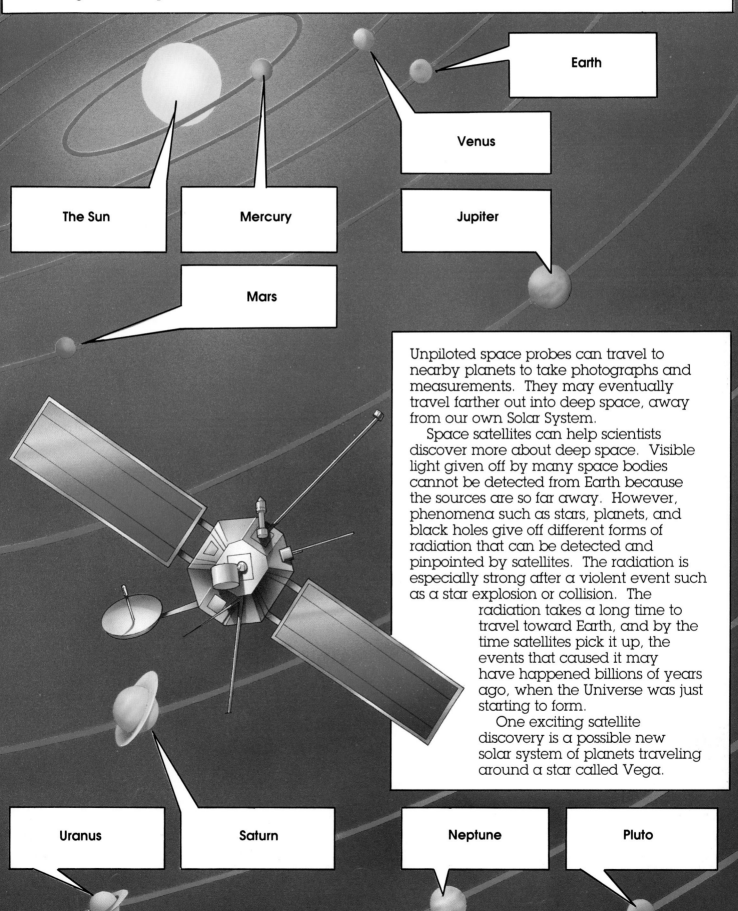

Earth

Venus

The Sun

Mercury

Jupiter

Mars

Unpiloted space probes can travel to nearby planets to take photographs and measurements. They may eventually travel farther out into deep space, away from our own Solar System.

Space satellites can help scientists discover more about deep space. Visible light given off by many space bodies cannot be detected from Earth because the sources are so far away. However, phenomena such as stars, planets, and black holes give off different forms of radiation that can be detected and pinpointed by satellites. The radiation is especially strong after a violent event such as a star explosion or collision. The radiation takes a long time to travel toward Earth, and by the time satellites pick it up, the events that caused it may have happened billions of years ago, when the Universe was just starting to form.

One exciting satellite discovery is a possible new solar system of planets traveling around a star called Vega.

Uranus

Saturn

Neptune

Pluto

SPACE STATIONS

A space station is a satellite with a crew on board. So far, space stations have stayed in orbit for only a few years at a time. Future stations are likely to orbit permanently.

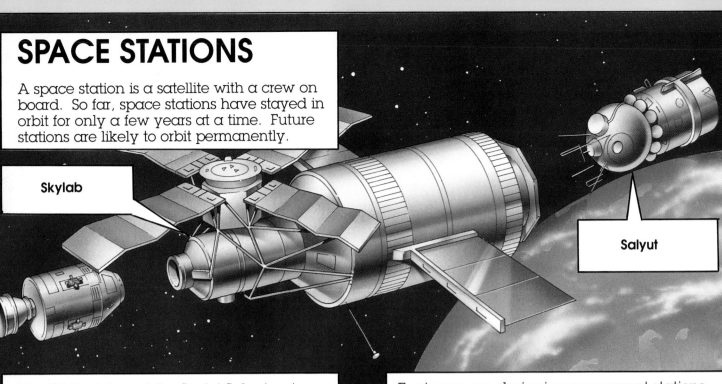

Skylab

Salyut

The US Skylab and the Soviet Salyut series were the first space stations to orbit for long periods of time. In both stations the crews did important work, studying the effects of living in space, performing experiments, and surveying the Earth.

Engineers are designing permanent stations to be built in space, using shuttle-type craft. They will probably consist of several modules connected by metal beams containing computer and power links. The stations will act as space observatories and factories.

SPACE SHUTTLES

The space shuttle can be used again and again. It is launched like a rocket, using boosters that are jettisoned after takeoff. It can land under its own power.

This type of craft could ferry crews and equipment to the new permanent space stations. The shuttle has a robot arm that could be used to build the stations.

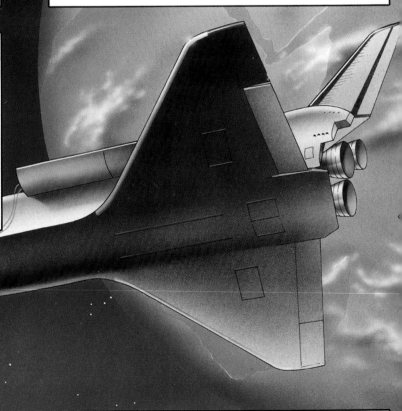

Some products that are hard to make on Earth can be more easily manufactured in space because there is no gravity there. These include very pure medicines, crystals, and metal mixtures. It's possible to stretch floating, weightless liquid into sheets to form perfect lens shapes. Companies may rent areas of space stations to manufacture these products free of gravity.

Living in space has problems that are yet to be solved. For instance, when someone is weightless, body fluids move upward, making the face puffy and causing symptoms similar to a bad cold. Regular exercise is essential to keep body muscles from growing weak. People also grow slightly taller because gravity no longer pulls on their spine.

SPACE FACT FINDER

Space greenhouses may be part of future space stations. Not only will these provide fresh food, but the plants will absorb some of the carbon dioxide breathed out by the crew. Liquid nutrients would circulate around the plant roots in place of soil.

An antenna farm is one idea for meeting communication demands. It is an enormous array of antennas attached together on a beam structure in space.

There are plans for a satellite that will be able to probe the Earth's upper atmosphere for study purposes. To prevent gravity from pulling it down to a lower orbit, a shuttle will tow it on a long tether.

Space telescopes, launched above the atmosphere from shuttles, will enable astronomers to see up to seven times farther than the best telescopes on Earth. They may discover new galaxies and planets.

Space is a very busy place! There are about 5,000 satellites in orbit, and there is a lot of space hardware floating around too. This includes old rocket stages, nuts, bolts, and even an astronaut's glove!

The first satellite was Sputnik 1, launched in 1957. About the size of a beach ball, it worked for 23 days. Today's satellites may be as large as a two-story house and last for up to ten years.

Satellites and space stations must have strong shells to withstand impacts from flying space debris, such as meteorites.

FUTURE SCIENCE

Scientific research now in progress will eventually lead to discoveries and inventions that will shape the technology of the future and affect our everyday lives. This section explains a few of the possibilities.

SUPERCONDUCTIVITY

Superconductivity is a new scientific principle that will make electricity much cheaper and more efficient.

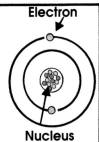

Electrons move around the nucleus of an atom. These electrons carry a negative electric charge.

Different types of material contain different numbers of electrons inside their atoms.

Electron

Nucleus

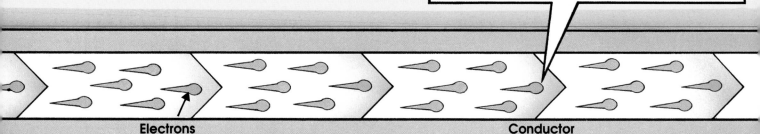

Electrons

Conductor

Heat generated

An electric current consists of electrons flowing through a material that conducts it. Electrons are tiny parts of atoms (see p. 12). When they travel through conducting material, they generate an electric current. As they move they lose energy, which turns to heat.

Scientists can measure the conductivity of a material to find out if it is a good or a poor conductor. Good conductors have a large number of freely moving electrons. Poor conductors have few or no electrons free to move. They can act as insulators.

Poor conductors

Conducting wire

Some materials, such as metals, are good conductors. Electrons flow easily through good conductors and do not need to use up much energy in order to move. This is why electricity-carrying cables are made of metal.

Materials such as wood, rubber, glass, and china are poor conductors. Electrons must expend large amounts of energy to move through them at all. They are good insulators.

In 1911, a scientist named Heike Kamerlingh Onnes made a discovery. When he cooled mercury down to -452°F (-269°C), the electrons in the metal used hardly any energy at all in order to move. Onnes had turned a good conductor into a superconductor.

Up to now, superconductivity use has been limited. Few materials can be used, and it is difficult to cool them to the very low temperatures needed to make them into superconductors.

USING THE DISCOVERY

Recently, scientists have found new super-conducting materials that do not need to be made as cold as mercury.

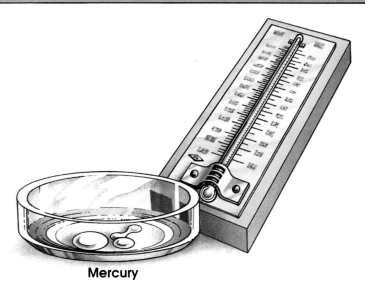

Mercury

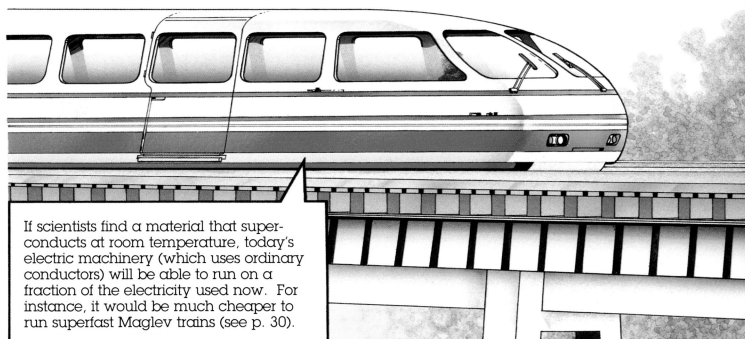

If scientists find a material that super-conducts at room temperature, today's electric machinery (which uses ordinary conductors) will be able to run on a fraction of the electricity used now. For instance, it would be much cheaper to run superfast Maglev trains (see p. 30).

(see p. 30)

Computers built with superconductors would run on much less electricity and work more efficiently than today's models. It might be possible to build superfast computers that are very cheap to run.

Very small amounts of energy could move enormous electric currents through superconducting power cables.

This means that electricity could become a cheaper and more abundant form of energy in the future.

GENETIC FINGERPRINTS

Genetic patterns, or fingerprints, are present in every human cell. They could well be the key to future crime detection because it is impossible to hide them.

Every living cell contains chromosome pairs that determine characteristics such as eye and hair color. The information stored inside the chromosomes is different for every person.

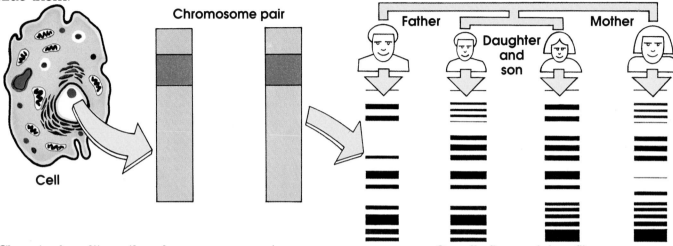

Cell

Chromosome pair

Father **Daughter and son** **Mother**

Genetic fingerprint on film

Chemicals split up the chromosome parts that hold genetic information. Other chemicals that affect film mark the pieces. The marked pieces are placed next to film that is then developed to show a genetic fingerprint made up of bands.

Genetic fingerprints can identify a person's real parents or children. Half of a child's genetic information will be the same as the father's, and half will be the same as the mother's. This system already has been used to reveal dog pedigrees.

HOLOGRAMS

Hologram 3-D images (see p. 20) may be more commonly used in the future for art, in advertising, and in decorating the home.

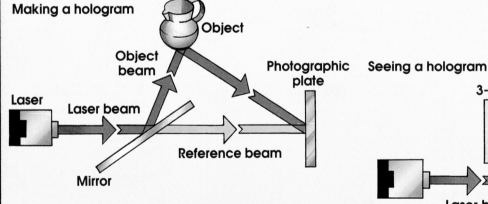

Making a hologram

Object

Object beam

Photographic plate

Laser

Laser beam

Reference beam

Mirror

Seeing a hologram

3-D image

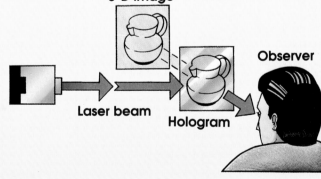

Observer

Laser beam

Hologram

1. A laser beam travels to a mirror that splits it into a reference beam and an object beam.

2. The object beam bounces off an object onto a photographic plate. A mirror or prism reflects the reference beam to the same photographic plate.

3. The two beams produce patterns on the photographic film. This is the hologram.

4. When light falls on the hologram, you see the patterns from both beams. The eye can't tell them apart, so the object seems to be behind the picture surface in 3-D.

TIME DILATION

Time dilation is the term used for describing the phenomena of time passing more slowly. Scientists have proved that this could actually happen, but only for things traveling nearly as fast as the speed of light.

In the distant future, spaceships might travel at these speeds, and astronauts who went on space journeys might return to find their children older than themselves! Time would have traveled more slowly for them than for people on Earth.

If time dilation proves possible, it could be useful. For instance, space hospitals, traveling at near light speed, could care for people with incurable diseases, providing more time to find a cure.

Time dilation could benefit exploration into deep space. High-speed travel, plus time passing more slowly, would allow the crew to finish its journey of exploration within the astronauts' lifetimes.

FOR MORE INFORMATION

MAGAZINES

Here are some children's magazines that have had recent articles about the world of the future. Look for them at your library, or write to the publishers listed below for information about subscribing.

Current Science
Field Publications
4343 Equity Drive
Columbus, OH 43228

National Geographic World
National Geographic Society
P.O. Box 2330
Washington, DC 20013-9865

Odyssey
Kalmbach Publishing Co.
21027 Crossroads Circle
Waukesha, WI 53186

Science World
Scholastic, Inc.
P.O. Box 644
Lyndhurst, NJ 07071-9985

Scienceland
Scienceland, Inc.
501 Fifth Ave.
New York, NY 10017-6165

ADDRESSES

The organizations listed below have information about the world of the future. When you write to them, tell them exactly what you want to know. Be sure to include your full name, age, and address.

Alternative Energy Resources Organization
324 Fuller - C4
Helena, MT 59601

National Aeronautics and Space Administration
Office of Aeronautics and Space Technology
NASA Headquarters
Washington, DC 20546

National Science Foundation
Directorate for Scientific, Technological,
and International Affairs
Division of Industrial Science and
Technological Innovation
1800 G St., NW
Washington, DC 20550

BOOKS

The following books will give you more information about exciting changes ahead in the world of the future. Look for them in your local library, or ask someone to order them for you at a bookstore.

Artificial Intelligence. (Silver Burdett)
Computers at Home: Today and Tomorrow. Darling (Dillon)
Computers in Your Life. Berger (Harper Jr.)
Experimenting with Energy. Ward (David & Charles)
Exploring with Computers. Bitter (Messner)
The Future World of Energy. Grolier Editors and Douglas (Franklin Watts)
Gifts from Space: How Space Technology Is Improving Life on Earth. Taylor (Harper Jr.)
Looking at Medicine. Sully (David & Charles)
Medical Technology. Wickham (Franklin Watts)
Medicine. Durie (Silver Burdett)
Medicine in the Future. Lambert (Franklin Watts)
On the Brink of Tomorrow: Frontiers of Science. Crump, editor (National Geographic)
Robotics. Potter and Guild (EDC)
Small Energy Sources: Choices That Work. Goldin (Harcourt Brace Jovanovich)
Space: Battleground of the Future? Taylor (Franklin Watts)
Space Exploration. (Boy Scouts of America)
Technology. Fox (David & Charles)
World of the Future. Gatland and Jeffries (EDC)

GLOSSARY

Algae
A group of simple plantlike organisms having no roots, stems, or leaves, which live in damp or moist places.

Atom
The smallest particle of any element.

Diagnosis
The recognition or naming of a disease from its outward signs, or symptoms.

Electron
A very small charge of negative electricity, often forming one part of an atom.

Endoscope
An instrument for examining visually the inside of a hollow organ of the body.

Fission
The splitting of the nucleus of an atom, resulting in the release of large amounts of energy and radioactivity.

Generator
A machine that produces an electric charge.

Geyser
A spring from which high columns of steam and boiling water rise into the air at certain, often regular, intervals.

Helium
A colorless, gaseous chemical element separated from the natural gases because it does not burn.

Hologram
A three-dimensional picture made by using laser lights and mirrors.

Hydrogen
A gaseous element, colorless, odorless, tasteless, and lighter than any other known substance.

Innovation
A change made by bringing in or introducing something new.

Laser
A device that uses the natural movements of atoms to enlarge or generate light waves.

Methane
An odorless, flammable gas produced by the decomposition of vegetable or organic matter in marshes and mines; it can be used as a fuel.

Nucleus
The central portion of an atom, containing a positive charge.

Petroleum
A raw oil obtained from wells drilled in the ground and prepared for use in such forms as gasoline, kerosene, and fuel oils.

Radiation
The process in which energy in the forms of rays of light or heat is sent out from atoms and molecules as they undergo internal change.

Reservoir
A place where something is stored for use, most usually in a large quantity.

Robot
A machine designed and made to act somewhat like a living person.

Sewage
Waste liquids and solid matter carried off by special underground drains.

Solar
Produced or operated by the Sun's heat.

Sterile
Free from living germs; disinfected.

Technology
The science that deals with practical or industrial arts; applied science.

Turbine
An engine or motor driven by the pressure of steam, water, or air against a set of blades that is attached to a driving shaft.

INDEX